TORNADO

by Jessica Rudolph

Consultant:
Dr. Charles A. Doswell III
Doswell Scientific Consulting
NOAA Severe Storms Scientist (retired)

BEARPORT
PUBLISHING

New York, New York

Credits

Cover, © iStockphoto/Thinkstock; 4–5, © AFP/Getty Images; 6–7, © iStockphoto/Thinkstock; 8–9, © Eric Nguyen/Jim Reed Photography; 9T, © Mike Theiss; 9B, © Willoughby Owen; 10–11, © Pete Draper; 12–13, © Stockbyte/Thinkstock; 12, © Martin Haas; 14–15, © AP Photo/ Wynter Byrd; 16–17, © Mr. T in DC; 17, © Associated Press; 18–19, © FEMA/Alamy; 20–21, © Reuters/Eric Thayer; 20, © AP Photo/Journal Times, Scott Anderson; 22, © Minerva Studio/ Shutterstock; 23TL, © Associated Press; 23TR, © FEMA/Alamy; 23BL, © Eric Nguyen/Jim Reed Photography; 23BR, © Mr. T in DC.

Publisher: Kenn Goin
Creative Director: Spencer Brinker
Design: Debrah Kaiser
Photo Researcher: Michael Win

Library of Congress Cataloging-in-Publication Data

Rudolph, Jessica.
  Tornado / by Jessica Rudolph.
      pages cm — (It's a disaster!)
  Includes index.
  ISBN 978-1-62724-126-7 (library binding) — ISBN 1-62724-126-4 (library binding)
  1. Tornadoes—Juvenile literature. I. Title.
  QC955.2.R834 2014
  551.55'3—dc23
                                    2013032436

For more information, write to Bearport Publishing Company, Inc., 45 West 21st Street, Suite 3B, New York, New York 10010. Printed in the United States of America.

10 9 8 7 6 5 4 3 2

CONTENTS

TORNADOES

Whoosh!

Strong winds start
to blow.

Dirt and branches
fly through the air.

A **tornado** is coming!

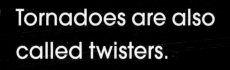

Tornadoes are also called twisters.

The winds move faster and faster in a circle.

Crack!

They pull a giant tree out of the ground!

Tornado winds can sound like a large waterfall.

A tornado is a powerful storm.

It is a huge tower of air that spins in a circle.

Tornadoes come in different shapes. They can be wide or thin.

A tornado's winds can reach 300 miles per hour (483 kph)!

Winds this fast can destroy buildings.

Tornado winds are faster than the winds of any other storm.

Sometimes, twisters flatten houses.

Sometimes, they toss cars through the air.

Tornadoes can peel roads up from the ground.

Tornadoes are scary!

Many people have been hurt or even killed by them.

Twisters can suck people into the air. People can also be hit by flying objects.

How can you stay safe?

Check **weather reports**.

They will tell you if a tornado is coming.

Find weather reports on TV or the Internet.

If a tornado is near, find **shelter** right away!

The safest place is a basement or **storm cellar**.

Underground shelters keep you safe from flying objects.

19

During a tornado, cover your head with your hands.

Stay in your shelter until the twister is gone.

After a tornado, people clean up the mess.

TORNADO FACTS

- Twisters stretch from the sky down to the ground.

- Tornadoes happen during thunderstorms. Thunderstorms have dark clouds, rain, thunder, and lightning.

- Tornadoes can happen any time of the year. They can last a few seconds or several hours.

- Twisters may travel for more than 200 miles (322 km).

GLOSSARY

shelter (SHEL-tur) a place that provides safety from danger

storm cellar (STORM SEL-ur) an underground room people go to for protection from storms

tornado (tor-NAY-doh) a powerful spinning tower of air that moves over land and can cause much destruction

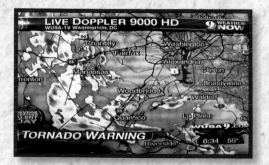

weather reports (WETH-ur rih-PORTS) reports that tell what the weather will be like in the coming hours or days

INDEX

READ MORE

Chambers, Catherine. *Tornado (Wild Weather).* Chicago: Heinemann (2002).

Gibbons, Gail. *Tornadoes!* New York: Holiday House (2009).

LEARN MORE ONLINE

To learn more about tornadoes, visit
www.bearportpublishing.com/ItsaDisaster!

ABOUT THE AUTHOR

Jessica Rudolph lives in Connecticut. She has edited and written many books about history, science, and nature for children.